DINOSAURS!

ANKYLOSAURUS
AND OTHER ARMOURED AND
PLATED HERBIVORES

by
David West

W

FRANKLIN WATTS
LONDON • SYDNEY

First published in the UK in 2013 by Franklin Watts

Franklin Watts
338 Euston Road
London NW1 3BH

Franklin Watts Australia
Level 17/207 Kent Street
Sydney, NSW 2000

Dewey classification: 567.9'15

A CIP catalogue record for this book is available from the British Library.

ISBN: 978 1 4451 2733 0

Franklin Watts is a division of Hachette Children's Books, an Hachette UK company.
www.hachette.co.uk

DINOSAURS! ANKYLOSAURUS and other ARMOURED and PLATED HERBIVORES
was produced for Franklin Watts by
David West Children's Books, 7 Princeton Court, 55 Felsham Road, London SW15 1AZ

Designed and illustrated by David West

Printed in China

Contents

TAIL CLUBS
Some **ankylosaurs** had tail clubs that were used as a defensive weapon. **Stegosaurs** often had spikes at the end of their tail that were used for the same purpose.

What Are Armoured and Plated **Herbivores**?

Many plant-eating dinosaurs were too slow to run from **predators**. Instead, they relied on heavy armour in the form of thick skin and bony plates. Mostly it was ankylosaurs and stegosaurs that had armour plating. There were also some large **sauropods** known as **titanosaurs** that had armour, as well as some frilled dinosaurs such as *Stegoceras*, which had an armoured skull.

*Dinosaurs lived throughout the Mesozoic Era, which is divided into three periods, shown here. It is sometimes called the Age of the Reptiles. Dinosaurs first appeared in the Upper Triassic period and died out during a **mass extinction event** 65 million years ago.*

ARMOUR
The tough, leathery skin was punctured by plates, spikes, and nodules called **osteoderms**. These bony growths grew from the skin layer and were not attached to the skeleton.

SMALL HEADS
Common to all these armoured dinosaurs was the size of their heads, which were small compared with their bodies. Their brains were also very small.

BEAK
Both ankylosaurs and stegosaurs had beaks with which they cropped plants such as ferns and **cycads**. **Batteries** of leaf-shaped teeth mashed up the plants gathered in their cheeks before they swallowed.

SIZE
These dinosaurs varied in size and weight, and are compared with a man in armour throughout the book.

FOUR-LEGGED
These armoured dinosaurs walked on four strong, sturdy legs.

This is the armoured dinosaur Ankylosaurus. It is the most famous of all ankylosaurs (see pp. 8–9).

	227		205		180		159	144			98		65 Millions of years ago (mya)
	Upper	Lower		Middle		Upper		Lower			Upper		
	TRIASSIC			JURASSIC				CRETACEOUS					

Ampelosaurus

Ampelosaurus means 'vineyard lizard', referring to where its fossils were found. It is a type of sauropod called a titanosaur. Like most sauropods, it had a long neck and tail but, unlike the majority of sauropods, it also had armour in the form of osteoderms on its back.

Most titanosaurs had some armour in the form of **nodules** and spikes of osteoderms on their backs. One species, *Saltasaurus*, had bony plates like those on *Ankylosaurus* (see pp. 8–9). *Ampelosaurus*'s

6

*A pair of adult Ampelosauruses and a **juvenile** take a rest on a beach while **migrating** to summer feeding grounds in this scene from Upper Cretaceous Europe. Experts know they were armoured from skin impressions found with the **fossils**.*

armour was not as spectacular as the armour on the ankylosaurs. However, it must have been helpful as a defence against predators such as **dromaeosaurs**, which hunted in packs. *Ampelosaurus* was a plant eater and used its needle-like teeth to strip leaves from the branches of trees. It may have reared up on its hind legs to reach the highest branches, using its tail as a balance.

Ampelosaurus was about 15 metres (49.2 feet) long and weighed around 9 metric tons (10 tons).

Ankylosaurus

Ankylosaurus, or 'fused lizard', gets its name from the oval plates embedded (fused) in its leathery skin. The group of dinosaurs that share similar armour take their name from *Ankylosaurus* and are called ankylosaurs. *Ankylosaurus* was the last armoured dinosaur to **evolve**.

Its entire top side was heavily protected from **carnivores** with thick, leathery skin from which grew bony, oval plates of osteoderms. Four large, triangular horns grew from the back of its head, the top of

8

*A small group of Ankylosauruses move slowly through low-lying vegetation in this scene from Upper Cretaceous North America. They **graze** on bushes and ferns with their beaks, using their small, leaf-shaped teeth to mash up the food.*

which was plated. It even had bony plates on its eyelids to protect its eyes. At the end of its tail was a large, bony club. *Ankylosaurus* could use its tail club as a defensive weapon, swinging it at the legs of attackers such as *Tyrannosaurus*, *Tarbosaurus*, and *Deinonychus*. Its only weak point was its underside, and it could only be defeated if an attacker managed to flip it on to its back.

Ankylosaurus was about 7 metres (23 feet) long and weighed around 5.3 metric tons (5.8 tons).

Crichtonsaurus

Crichtonsaurus is named after the author Michael Crichton, who wrote *Jurassic Park*. *Crichtonsaurus* was a **nodosaur**, a member of the ankylosaurs. Strangely, though, it had small, flat, bony plates sticking upwards from its back, similar to a stegosaur.

Crichtonsaurus, like all nodosaurs, had no tail club with which to defend itself. It was a smallish dinosaur that walked on all four legs with its body close to the ground. It had a parrot-like beak to crop plants

10

Two Crichtonsauruses *move away from a small lake as an electrical storm approaches.*
A *startled* Probactrosaurus *looks up from the edge of the lake in this scene from Upper Cretaceous Asia.*

and a battery of teeth to mash up its food. It had a small head that contained a small brain, and it probably spent most of its time grazing like modern-day cows. It lived in wooded areas of fir trees and ferns that were criss-crossed by rivers and lakes. *Crichtonsaurus* may have lived in small herds for added protection.

Crichtonsaurus was 3 metres (9.8 feet) long and weighed 0.9 metric ton (1 ton).

Upper Jurassic
154–150 mya
England, France, Portugal, Spain

Dacentrurus

Dacentrurus, meaning 'pointed tail', was the first stegosaur ever found. The tail spikes were very sharp and would have made excellent defensive weapons against *Metriacanthosaurus* and other large predators of the time.

Although *Dacentrurus* was a small to medium-sized stegosaur, some fossil discoveries suggest that some individuals grew to larger sizes. Some may have been as big as *Stegosaurus* (see pp. 24–25).

Using its sharp, spiked tail, Dacentrurus defends itself from an attack by a Metriacanthosaurus, *which has received a nasty slashing wound to its neck in this scene from Upper Jurassic Europe.*

Dacentrurus was common across Europe during the Upper Jurassic. No fossils have been found outside this area, whereas *Stegosaurus* appeared in North America as well as Europe. This suggests that some stegosaur **species** were more wide-ranging than others. *Stegosaurus* and *Dacentrurus* might have **co-existed**.

Dacentrurus grew up to 6 metres (19.7 feet) long and weighed about 1.8 metric tons (2 tons).

Euoplocephalus

Euoplocephalus, meaning 'well-armoured head', is the most studied **ankylosaurid**. Over 40 fossils of this dinosaur have been found. Fewer than ten fossils have been found of its more famous cousin, *Ankylosaurus*. Much of what we know about *Ankylosaurus* is based on careful study of *Euoplocephalus*.

Euoplocephalus had all the features of an ankylosaur. It had a heavily armoured body and a slow, four-legged walk. Unusually, it had only

In this scene from Upper Cretaceous North America, a group of Euoplocephaluses gather at a water hole to drink. A Tyrannosaurus rex *lurks nearby, ready to pounce on any defenceless* **prey** *that may wander too far from the safety of its herd.*

three toes on each foot, whereas all other ankylosaurs had four or five toes. It was a member of the ankylosaurids, a subgroup of ankylosaurs that had tail clubs. The club was used as a defence against predators. If attacked, *Euoplocephalus* would quickly position itself facing away from the predator and swing its bone-smashing club at the enemy's legs.

Euoplocephalus grew up to 7 metres (23 feet) long and weighed up to 3.6 metric tons (4 tons).

15

Upper Jurassic
155–150 mya
Tanzania

Kentrosaurus

Kentrosaurus, or 'spiky lizard', gets its name from the many spikes sticking out of its back, tail and sides. It was a small stegosaurid compared with *Stegosaurus* (see pp. 24–25), reaching 1.5 metres (5 feet) in height.

Bony plates grew upwards from the front half of *Kentrosaurus*'s neck and back. Long, sharp spikes replaced the plates about halfway down its back and ran to the end of its tail. The longest spikes pointed out from the end of its tail. There was also a long spike growing outwards

Two Kentrosauruses graze on low-lying ferns, unaware that they are being watched by a Ceratosaurus in this scene from Upper Jurassic Africa. It is unlikely that a lone Ceratosaurus would take on two dinosaurs with such sizeable defences.

from its shoulder on each side. These scary-looking weapons were an effective defence against predators such as *Elaphrosaurus* and other **Tendaguru** carnivores. *Kentrosaurus* was a herbivore, and it grazed on low-lying shrubs, cycads, and ferns. Fossils show its teeth were leaf-like, ideal for cropping and mashing up the plants before swallowing them.

Kentrosaurus grew to 4.6 metres (15 feet) long and weighed about 1.4 metric tons (1.5 tons).

Lexovisaurus

Lexovisaurus, meaning 'Lexovii lizard', was named after the Lexovii, an ancient tribe from western Europe. It was one of the earliest European stegosaurs, a medium-sized herbivore that browsed the low-lying vegetation of modern-day France and England.

Lexovisaurus had a number of flat plates and rounded, pointed spines that ran along its back and tail. It also had spikes sticking outwards from its shoulders, similar to those on *Kentrosaurus* but larger.

A lone Lexovisaurus *grazes on low-lying plants among a herd of Cetiosauruses in this scene from Middle Jurassic Europe. Lone animals may have sought the protection of another dinosaur herd, especially if they did not compete for food.*

Lexovisaurus was once thought to belong to the *Dacentrurus* group, but it has since been given its own grouping in the stegosaur family. Like other stegosaurs, it spent its life browsing on low-lying plants such as ferns and cycads. It may have lived in herds or small family groups for protection from predators.

Lexovisaurus was around 8.2 metres (27 feet) long and weighed about 2 metric tons (2.2 tons).

19

**Lower Cretaceous
125 mya
England**

Polacanthus

Polacanthus means 'many spines'. It was an early armoured, plant-eating ankylosaur with many spikes protruding from its back, tail and sides. It had a large, single sheet of hard skin over its hips that was not attached to the underlying skeleton.

Polacanthus's armour plating with spikes was perfect protection against hungry predators who, if they got past the spikes, would find it difficult to penetrate the tough, hard dermal plates. As with

In a scene from Lower Cretaceous Europe, a couple of Polacanthuses *move away from a river's edge as a* Baryonyx *appears. The* Baryonyx *is hunting for fish and is unlikely to take on such well-armoured prey as* Polacanthus.

Crichtonsaurus (see pp. 10–11), it was first seen as a member of the nodosaurs, which did not have a tail club. Today, experts think it was probably a very primitive ankylosaurid. Like all ankylosaurs, it had a shuffling, four-legged walk. Its body was close to the ground and it fed on low-lying plants, which it cropped with its parrot-like beak. It lived alongside predators such as *Baryonyx.*

Polacanthus was about 5 metres (16.4 feet) long and weighed over 1.8 metric tons (2 tons).

Stegoceras

Stegoceras means 'horny roof'. The name refers to the dome on its head, which was 7.6 centimetres (3 inches) thick. Males had thicker domes than females, and the older a *Stegoceras*, the thicker the dome. There was a fringe of **horny** knobs along the rear of its skull.

It was once thought that *Stegocerases* (and other **pachycephalosaurs**) used their thick domes to head-butt rivals during mating displays, the way bighorn sheep do today, and also as a defence against predators.

In a dispute over territory, two male Stegocerases settle their differences by **flank**-butting each other in this scene from Upper Cretaceous North America. Evidence has shown their thick skulls were too **fragile** for head-to-head butting.

However, experts now think the dome's rounded shape would have resulted in glancing blows. Experiments have also shown the thick bone was not rigid and solid, but **porous** and fragile under pressure. **Paleontologists** now think that, instead of hitting each other head-on, Stegocerases flank-butted each other. Stegoceras lived in the hot, dry interior of what is now North America.

Stegoceras grew to about 2.1 metres (7 feet) long and weighed up to 77 kilogrammes (170 pounds).

23

Stegosaurus

Stegosaurus means 'roof lizard'. It was named for the large plates on its back, which were first thought to have lain flat on its back like roof tiles. A group of related dinosaurs take their name from *Stegosaurus* and are called stegosaurs.

Stegosaurus had a distinctive posture, with a heavily rounded back, short front legs, head held low to the ground, and a stiffened tail held high in the air. At the end of the tail were two sets of spikes, which

24

A *mother* Stegosaurus *protects her young from an attack by a trio of* Allosauruses *in this scene from Upper Jurassic North America. Fossil evidence has uncovered* Allosaurus *tail bones with punctures that perfectly fit* Stegosaurus *tail spikes.*

were used in defence against predators such as *Allosaurus* and *Ceratosaurus*. The large plates along its back were osteoderms, similar to those seen in crocodiles and some lizards today. They were not attached to its skeleton, but grew from its skin. Some experts think they helped control temperature; others think they were for courtship displays.

Stegosaurus was about 9 metres (29.5 feet) long and weighed up to 3.2 metric tons (3.5 tons).

Tuojiangosaurus

Tuojiangosaurus means 'Tuo River lizard'. Like *Stegosaurus,* it had long back legs and short front legs, as well as an arched back and a small head. Like other stegosaurs, *Tuojiangosaurus* had small teeth along the sides of the mouth; a relatively long, low snout; and a tiny brain.

Tuojiangosaurus had around 17 pairs of narrow, pointed plates. The last two pairs were thin, cone-shaped spines at the end of its tail. The

26

A thirsty Tuojiangosaurus *has waded into a lake to cool down and drink while* **primitive** *birds feed on flying insects in this scene from Upper Jurassic China. Lake shores were ideal places for predators to lie in wait for their prey.*

plates were low on the neck, grew bigger along the back, and then became smaller down the tail. There was also a large, plate-like spine above each shoulder. *Tuojiangosaurus* walked along riverbanks browsing on ferns and cycads. It cropped leaves with its beak, stuffed them into its cheeks, and chewed them between its small, ridged cheek teeth.

Tuojiangosaurus grew up to 7 metres (23 feet) long and weighed around 2.7 metric tons (3 tons).

27

Wuerhosaurus

Wuerhosaurus means 'lizard from Wuerho', a place in China. This large stegosaurid is one of the last plated dinosaurs to have survived. *Wuerhosaurus* had the spines and plates common to all stegosaurs, but they were **stumpier** than those of other stegosaurs.

Wuerhosaurus had a short neck and a low-slung posture with front legs shorter than the rear legs, which suggests that it fed on low-lying plants. *Wuerhosaurus* had short, rounded plates whose purpose is

28

Caked in salt from a dried-up salt lake, a mother Wuerhosaurus *and her baby call out to the rest of the herd. They became separated from their herd when winds whipped sand and salt into a dust storm in this scene from Lower Cretaceous Asia.*

uncertain. They were arranged in two rows and alternated. Some experts think they may have been used as a kind of temperature regulator; others think they were a form of armour. Like *Stegosaurus*, it had two sets of sharp spines on its tail. These were weapons of self-defence. By swinging its tail, it could seriously injure an attacking predator.

Wuerhosaurus grew up to 8 metres (26.2 feet) long and weighed up to 2 metric tons (2.2 tons).

Animal Gallery

Other dinosaurs and animals that appear in the scenes.

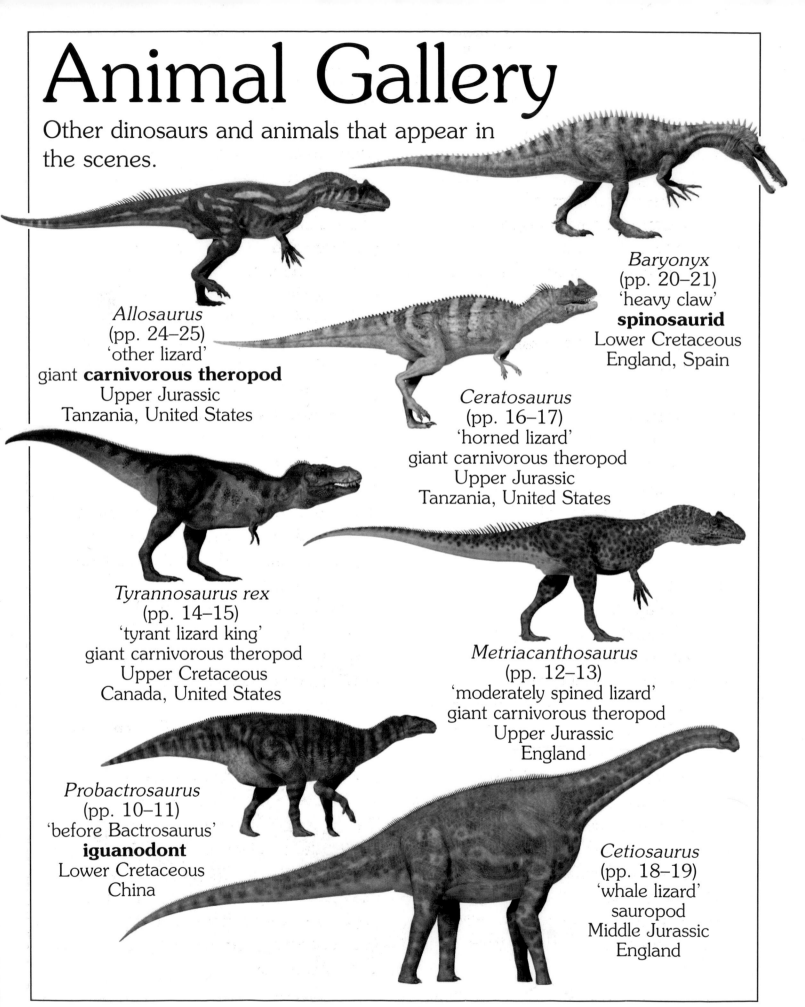

Baryonyx
(pp. 20–21)
'heavy claw'
spinosaurid
Lower Cretaceous
England, Spain

Allosaurus
(pp. 24–25)
'other lizard'
giant **carnivorous theropod**
Upper Jurassic
Tanzania, United States

Ceratosaurus
(pp. 16–17)
'horned lizard'
giant carnivorous theropod
Upper Jurassic
Tanzania, United States

Tyrannosaurus rex
(pp. 14–15)
'tyrant lizard king'
giant carnivorous theropod
Upper Cretaceous
Canada, United States

Metriacanthosaurus
(pp. 12–13)
'moderately spined lizard'
giant carnivorous theropod
Upper Jurassic
England

Probactrosaurus
(pp. 10–11)
'before Bactrosaurus'
iguanodont
Lower Cretaceous
China

Cetiosaurus
(pp. 18–19)
'whale lizard'
sauropod
Middle Jurassic
England

Glossary

ankylosaurid A member of the ankylosaur group that has a tail club.

ankylosaurs Members of a group of plant-eating dinosaurs with a low, thick body and armour.

batteries Rows or a grouping in lines.

carnivores Animals that eat meat.

carnivorous Meat-eating.

co-existed Lived at the same time.

cycads A kind of palm.

dromaeosaurs Members of a group of carnivorous dinosaurs known as raptors, with slashing claws on their feet.

evolve Gradually change by natural selection over a long period of time.

flank The side of an animal.

fossils The remains of living things that have turned to rock.

fragile Delicate nature and easily damaged.

graze To feed on growing plants.

herbivores Plant eaters.

horny Rough, knobbly skin.

iguanodont One of the group of plant-eating dinosaurs that includes *Iguanodon*.

juvenile A youngster.

mass extinction event A large disappearance of species of animals and plants in a relatively short period of time.

migrating Moving from one place to another, either for a short seasonal period or for ever.

nodosaur A member of the family of ankylosaurian dinosaurs that have no tail club.

nodules Small, rounded bumps.

osteoderms Bony deposits forming scales, plates, or other structures in layers of the skin.

pachycephalosaurs Members of a family of bone-headed dinosaurs that includes *Pachycephalosaurus*.

paleontologists Scientists who study the forms of life that existed in earlier geologic periods by looking at fossils.

porous Full of tiny holes or pores.

predators Animals that hunt and kill other animals for food.

prey An animal that is hunted by carnivores.

primitive An early form of something.

sauropods Members of a group of large, plant-eating dinosaurs that had very long necks.

species A group of animals that can breed with one another.

stegosaurs Members of a family of plated dinosaurs that included *Stegosaurus*.

spinosaurid A member of a family of large, two-legged predators with elongated, crocodile-like skulls.

stumpier Shorter and thicker.

Tendaguru The Tendaguru beds are a fossil-rich formation in Tanzania.

theropod A member of a two-legged dinosaur family that includes most of the giant carnivorous dinosaurs.

titanosaur A member of a group of very large sauropods.

Index